THEN & NOW

# LEESBURG

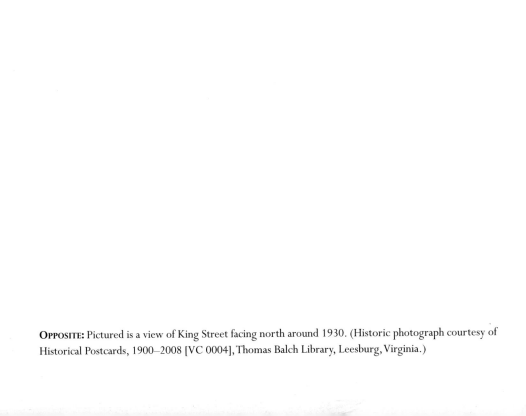

**OPPOSITE:** Pictured is a view of King Street facing north around 1930. (Historic photograph courtesy of Historical Postcards, 1900–2008 [VC 0004], Thomas Balch Library, Leesburg, Virginia.)

# LEESBURG

## Annie Laurie McDonald

*It is better to preserve than to restore, and better to restore than to reconstruct.*

*—A. N. Didron, 1839*

Library of Congress Control Number: 2010940817

Published by Arcadia Publishing
Charleston, South Carolina

Printed in the United States of America

For all general information, please contact Arcadia Publishing:
Telephone 843-853-2070
Fax 843-853-0044
E-mail sales@arcadiapublishing.com
For customer service and orders:
Toll-Free 1-888-313-2665

Visit us on the Internet at www.arcadiapublishing.com

ON THE FRONT COVER: People's National Bank is pictured around 1900. Today it is the Lightfoot Restaurant. See page 26 for more information. (Historic photograph courtesy of the Ethel Littlejohn Adams Photograph Collection [VC 0015], Thomas Balch Library, Leesburg, Virginia; now photograph by the author.)

ON THE BACK COVER: Dodona Manor is the former home of Gen. George C. Marshall. (Historic photograph courtesy of Historical Postcards, 1900–2008 [VC 0004], Thomas Balch Library, Leesburg, Virginia.)

# CONTENTS

Acknowledgments                                                          vii
Introduction                                                              ix

1.    Government, Education, and Public Buildings                          11

2.    The Economic and Social Center of Loudoun County                    21

3.    Leesburg's Manufacturing and Agricultural Heritage                   51

4.    Domestic and Religious Buildings                                     69

# ACKNOWLEDGMENTS

This book has been simmering for the past five years as Brian Boucher and I shared thoughts over the water cooler on Leesburg's evolution. I don't think either of us truly understood the extent of the change.

I am indebted to several individuals and organizations for their assistance in the preparation of this book. Pam Stewart, formerly with the Loudoun Museum, and Paul McCray at the Northern Virginia Regional Park Authority were extremely giving of their time and effort in selecting photographs for the book. Beth Schuster, formerly with the Thomas Balch Library, had a yeoman's task of compiling the majority of the photographs and responding to my frequent, scattered, and nonsensical requests. I am also grateful for the generosity of the Town of Leesburg's Department of Planning & Zoning, which permitted me to use photographs from the town's architectural survey files. Thanks to everyone who assisted with the preparation of this book.

Finally, this book would not have been possible without the generations of people who have built and preserved Leesburg's rich history and architectural heritage. In every beautiful town, there is a preservationist to thank. In Leesburg, there are many.

All current images are courtesy of the author.

# INTRODUCTION

Established in 1758 as the seat of Loudoun County, Leesburg's early development centered on what is known as the Nicholas Minor Section of town. This eight-block area was the heart of Loudoun County and an important crossroads community on the Old Carolina Road and the east-west routes connecting Alexandria to Winchester and Harpers Ferry. Leesburg prospered and grew in size and importance following the Revolutionary War, with many of the buildings in the historic core dating to the late 18th and early 19th centuries.

Leesburg experienced a second phase of growth following the Civil War. The easy access to rail transportation enabled Leesburg to further establish its authority as a center for trading and commerce, which fueled the town's agricultural and manufacturing development. The town's prosperity was evident in the size, quantity, and quality of the buildings throughout the town. Leesburg's steady growth continued through the early 20th century with little change to its character as a small but economically strong community.

The expansion of the federal government in the second and third quarters of the 20th century and the eventual creation of suburbs around Washington, DC, spurred further development in Leesburg beginning in the mid-1900s. Concerned about the loss of historic resources and the town's heritage, community leaders started a preservation movement. In 1949, Colonial Leesburg, Inc., formed to counteract the increasing modernization of the historic downtown. Taking cues from Williamsburg, this private, nonprofit organization led the efforts to give the town a more "Colonial" appearance. Colonial Leesburg's efforts, however, did not entirely prevent the loss of many historic buildings in the town.

In response to such demolitions and the increasing threat of new development as the Northern Virginia region expanded, in 1963, the town followed Alexandria's lead and passed an ordinance establishing the Old and Historic District. An important provision of the new ordinance was the stress placed on the preservation of buildings constructed prior to 1878—the date of the historic map used to identify the Historic District's boundaries. In the hierarchy, these structures were considered the most important. The buildings constructed after 1878 were most likely to be considered candidates for demolition or significant alterations. The ordinance has been modified since its first adoption—including the removal of the 1878 reference date. It is Leesburg's preservation ordinance, coupled with the community-minded spirit of its citizens, that has protected the majority of the resources in the Leesburg's historic core.

Then & Now: *Leesburg* explores the town's lost and extant structures and communicates the town's change over time. It gives equal consideration to grand structures like the Leesburg Inn and small buildings like the now-demolished house at 203 Liberty Street SW. It is easy to call to mind landmark buildings like the courthouse, Leesburg Inn, People's National Bank, and Leesburg Opera House. More remote to most people are the modest, vernacular structures that make up the bulk of the town's historic resources.

The chapters are arranged primarily by historic use and then by general area. The first two chapters include streetscapes and buildings that are well known to many. Chapter one explores publicly oriented structures, such as government and educational buildings, the county jail, and the hospital. Chapter two compares historic and current views of the commercial and cultural resources throughout the community. Although they include many well-known buildings, the last two chapters include some of the more obscure images of the town. This is particularly the case for chapter three, which looks at

Leesburg's industrial and agricultural heritage. Focused primarily on the area around Market Station, this chapter includes images that predate the redevelopment of this industrial area. Chapter four explores the historically residential parts of town.

By no means is this work all-inclusive. There are many buildings and streetscapes that are not represented. Neither is it meant to celebrate or mourn. It is intended instead to serve as a brief reminder of what once was.

# CHAPTER 1

# GOVERNMENT, EDUCATION, AND PUBLIC BUILDINGS

Constructed in 1888, the Loudoun County Jail included a jail yard, pictured at the right, as well as the sheriff's residence, pictured at the left. Though the jail was demolished in 1954 for construction of a new facility, the dwelling remained until the 1960s. (Historic photograph courtesy of the Winslow Williams Photograph Collection [VC 0003], Thomas Balch Library, Leesburg, Virginia.)

The current Loudoun County Courthouse is the third to be located on this site. Constructed in 1894, the building replaced the early-19th-century building pictured in the historic image below. The cupola surmounting the tower was recreated in the late 20th century after being blown off in a storm. (Historic photograph courtesy of the Thomas Balch Library Photograph Collection [VC 0001], Thomas Balch Library, Leesburg, Virginia.)

Constructed in the mid-1800s as an academy, the Greek Revival–style building to the left was sold to Loudoun County in the 1870s for use as the clerk's office. The addition to the right was built in the mid-1900s during an early expansion of the county government. The monumental entrance now bridging the two structures was added in the 1970s. (Historic photograph courtesy of the David Frye Photograph Collection [VC 0029], Thomas Balch Library, Leesburg, Virginia.)

GOVERNMENT, EDUCATION, AND PUBLIC BUILDINGS

Constructed in 1954, the south wing of the new jail (pictured at the right) was originally attached to the 1888 jailor's residence (page 11). The dwelling was demolished in 1966 to make way for a 1970 addition that more than doubled the jail's capacity. The building was demolished in 2009. (Historic photograph courtesy of the Town of Leesburg Department of Planning & Zoning.)

Though long since retired as a school, the current structure dates to the 1920s and is the third such building to be located on this site. Pictured below is the first school, which was constructed in the late 1800s and burned in the early 20th century. It was briefly replaced by a second school that burned shortly after construction. The current building now houses offices for Loudoun County. (Historic photograph courtesy of Historical Postcards, 1900–2008 [VC 0004], Thomas Balch Library, Leesburg, Virginia.)

Constructed around 1870, the structure known as Bailey's Institute served as one of the earliest African American schools in Leesburg. After the Civil War, there was no centralized school for the education of African American children in Leesburg, but there were several such independent schools in the town. The building later served as a church and social hall for Leesburg's African American residents. It was replaced with the current structure in the late 1970s. (Historic photograph courtesy of the Winslow Williams Photograph Collection [VC 0003], Thomas Balch Library, Leesburg, Virginia.)

GOVERNMENT, EDUCATION, AND PUBLIC BUILDINGS

Constructed in 1941 on land donated by African American residents in Loudoun County, Douglass High School was the only secondary school for African Americans until Loudoun County schools were desegregated in 1968–1969. Though basic furniture was provided by Loudoun County, the countywide league of all African American parent-teacher organizations purchased the majority of the furnishings and supplies. The building continues to serve as a community center operated by Loudoun County. (Historic photograph courtesy of the Winslow Williams Photograph Collection [VC 0003], Thomas Balch Library, Leesburg, Virginia.)

From 1912 to 1918, the Leesburg Hospital was located in the historic building at 9–11 West Market Street, which it quickly outgrew. In 1918, the new facility, renamed the Loudoun Hospital, was built on 13 acres near the intersection of Cornwall and Ayr Streets. The wing to the right was completed in 1949, and several additions followed. The hospital was eventually incorporated into the Inova Health System, and the structure now serves as an emergency care center. The expansion of the medical office building to the southwest was completed in 2007. (Historic photograph courtesy of the Winslow Williams Photograph Collection [VC 0003], Thomas Balch Library, Leesburg, Virginia.)

Located in the 1950s and 1960s in a converted dwelling at 12 Loudoun Street SW, the Town of Leesburg's offices expanded in the 1970s into a former garage located behind the Tally Ho Theatre (pictured below). The structure was built as an automobile sales-and-service center in the 1920s and then converted to a garage and repair shop by 1936. It served as the town hall until construction of the current facilities in 1990. (Historic photograph courtesy of the Charles A. Bos Photograph Collection [VC 0024], Thomas Balch Library, Leesburg, Virginia.)

Built to replace the outdated structure on page 19, Leesburg's current town hall was the product of a design competition initiated in the mid-1980s. The Illinois-based firm of Hanno Weber and Associates placed first in the competition with this design. The building occupies land that was, until the 1930s, home to a two-story brick dwelling of the early 19th century. (Historic photograph courtesy of the Thomas Balch Library Photograph Collection [VC 0001], Thomas Balch Library, Leesburg, Virginia.)

GOVERNMENT, EDUCATION, AND PUBLIC BUILDINGS

# CHAPTER 2

# THE ECONOMIC AND SOCIAL CENTER OF LOUDOUN COUNTY

Some documentation suggests that the original c. 1800 core of this series of buildings is the central three-bay-wide section facing West Market Street (behind the streetlight). The portion of the building facing South King Street is a later addition dating to the mid-1800s. In the mid-20th century, the building was home to Plaster's Clothing. The photograph above depicts the structure undergoing the first of three significant renovations. The building was modernized and clad in an Art Deco–inspired storefront. (Historic photograph courtesy of the Winslow Williams Photograph Collection [VC 0003], Thomas Balch Library, Leesburg, Virginia.)

This iconic view of North King Street dates to around 1900 and depicts many of the buildings prior to Colonial Revival–inspired renovations that began in the 1940s. The importance of King Street as a center for commerce is evident in the number of people passing by and mingling along the streetscape. (Historic photograph courtesy of the Thomas Balch Library Photograph Collection [VC 0002], Thomas Balch Library, Leesburg, Virginia.)

THE ECONOMIC AND SOCIAL CENTER OF LOUDOUN COUNTY

Constructed around 1830, the group of three storefronts at 1, 3, and 5 North King Street are among the earliest remaining purpose-built commercial buildings in Leesburg. They were stylistically updated in the late 1800s. In 1950, the southern and central structures were some of the first buildings to be renovated in accordance with the principles espoused by Colonial Leesburg, Inc. The multipaned display windows were added at that time. The building at 5 North King Street retains its late-19th-century storefront. (Historic photograph courtesy of the Winslow Williams Photograph Collection [VC 0003], Thomas Balch Library, Leesburg, Virginia.)

Occupied by Littlejohn's Drugs through the first half of the 20th century, the commercial building at 7 North King Street dates to around 1900. The arcaded, Colonial-inspired storefront dates to 1971, when the Virginia Savings and Loan Association occupied the building. (Historic photograph courtesy of the Ethel Littlejohn Adams Photograph Collection [VC 0015], Thomas Balch Library, Leesburg, Virginia.)

The structures at 9 and 11 North King Street have undergone significant changes over time. Contemporaries of the structures on page 23, these two buildings were modified in the late 1800s or early 1900s to incorporate wider windows on the first story. The building occupied by the *Loudoun News* in the mid-20th century was altered around 1950 to have a more Colonial appearance. (Historic photograph courtesy of the Winslow Williams Photograph Collection [VC 0003], Thomas Balch Library, Leesburg, Virginia.)

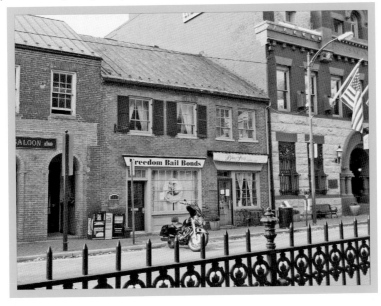

One of the most well-known landmarks in Leesburg, People's National Bank is also one of the largest extant commercial buildings in town. Originally constructed in the 1890s, it was enlarged in 1907 to its current form. The building continued to operate as a bank through the late 20th century. Renovated in the late 1990s with the benefit the federal and state rehabilitation tax credits, the building is now home to the Lightfoot Restaurant. (Historic photograph courtesy of the Ethel Littlejohn Adams Photograph Collection [VC 0015], Thomas Balch Library, Leesburg, Virginia.)

THE ECONOMIC AND SOCIAL CENTER OF LOUDOUN COUNTY

When originally built, People's National Bank was shorter and narrower than it is today. Sitting to the north of it was a modest, unadorned two-story commercial building (page 26). Once expanded, the bank building extended all the way to 15 North King Street, then an early-19th-century commercial building. Later demolished, this early structure at 15 North King Street was replaced in 1965 by the existing Colonial Revival–style building. (Historic photograph courtesy of the Ethel Littlejohn Adams Photograph Collection [VC 0015], Thomas Balch Library, Leesburg, Virginia.)

With its long, arcaded three-story porch, the 1894 Leesburg Inn framed the north side of the courthouse lawn. The structure continued to serve as an inn through the mid-20th century until it was purchased by Loudoun County for additional office space. The inn was later demolished in 1974 to make way for a new county office building. Due to the fact that the structure did not pre-date 1878, the then-members of the Leesburg Board of Architectural Review (BAR) "took no position on the proposed razing" (minutes of the BAR, 14 January 1974). (Historic photograph courtesy of the Winslow Williams Photograph Collection [VC 0003], Thomas Balch Library, Leesburg, Virginia.)

Constructed between 1930 and 1937, the original Esso station at the corner of Market and Wirt Streets was a modest representation of the Art Deco style. In 1967, the Humble Oil Company proposed demolition of the 1930s structure as well as the two dwellings to the west for construction of the current Colonial Revival–style gas station. The demolition was approved on the basis that the structures did not have "particular historical significance or architectural merit." (Historic photograph courtesy of the Winslow Williams Photograph Collection [VC 0003], Thomas Balch Library, Leesburg, Virginia.)

Dating to the 1790s, the tavern at 20 West Market Street was expanded in the 1830s or 1840s and subsequently used as a dwelling. The obvious seam in the masonry between the elaborate Greek Revival–style entrance and the rest of the building indicates this phase of alterations. The building was returned to use as an inn in the mid-20th century, as illustrated in the historic image above, and now serves as offices. (Historic photograph courtesy of the Winslow Williams Photograph Collection [VC 0003], Thomas Balch Library, Leesburg, Virginia.)

The Art Deco–style Tally Ho Theatre operated continually from 1931 until 2000, when it underwent a two-year renovation before opening again. The building originally included two commercial storefronts flanking the entrance. In the 1970s, the building was remodeled, with the commercial bays enclosed. The 2000–2002 renovation restored the western storefront to an appearance closely resembling the original design. Though built as a single-screen theater, the Tally Ho now features two screens. (Historic photograph courtesy of the Winslow Williams Photograph Collection [VC 0003], Thomas Balch Library, Leesburg, Virginia.)

The site at 10 West Market Street had been home to several commercial buildings before the construction of the current drive-through bank in 1975. As pictured here, three frame buildings occupied this site from the 1880s through the early 1900s. Though now used as commercial space, the extant three-story structure in the background was built in the 1890s as two adjoining townhouses. (Historic photograph courtesy of the Thomas Balch Library Photograph Collection [VC 0001], Thomas Balch Library, Leesburg, Virginia.)

In the 1920s, the three frame structures on page 32 were demolished to make way for Whitmore's Garage. The brick-clad hollow-tile structure was an automobile sales and service center and remained in use as an auto body shop through the late 1960s. It was later purchased by the nearby People's National Bank and ultimately demolished for the 1975 construction of the drive-through bank. (Historic photograph courtesy of the Thomas Balch Library Photograph Collection [VC 0001], Thomas Balch Library, Leesburg, Virginia.)

The Colonial Revival–style building at 9 East Market Street was built in 1916 as an automobile sales store for the Dodge Motor Company. Between 1935 and 1945, the building's use—but not appearance—changed as the Virginia Electric Power Company occupied it. By the 1960s, it was the home of the *Loudoun Times-Mirror*, which altered the building's facade in the late 20th century to its current configuration. (Historic photograph courtesy of the Winslow Williams Photograph Collection [VC 0003], Thomas Balch Library, Leesburg, Virginia.)

One of the most well-known historic images of King Street, this view facing south dates to the early 1900s, before the 1920s enlargement and renovation of the First National Bank. At that time, not only was the building modernized with a new exterior, it was given a third story. Although the 1920s stone veneer covered the mostly brick exterior, still visible from the original construction is the corbelled pediment over the entrance. (Historic photograph courtesy of the Town of Leesburg Records, Thomas Balch Library, Leesburg, Virginia.)

After its modernization in the 1950s (page 21), which resulted in a simplified Art Deco storefront on the building, Plaster's Clothing further modified the structure in 1971. This second phase of alterations gave the store a Colonial appearance, with multipaned storefront windows, a recessed entrance, and a sloping, metal-clad roof. The building was altered once again in 1990, when the storefront was returned to a design somewhat consistent with its late-19th-century appearance. It was also at this time that the north elevation was painted to delineate the different construction phases. (Historic photograph courtesy of the Town of Leesburg Department of Planning & Zoning.)

THE ECONOMIC AND SOCIAL CENTER OF LOUDOUN COUNTY

The structural glass (also known as Carrara glass) storefront at 5 South King Street is the only remaining expression of mid-century modernism of this type in downtown Leesburg. It was added to the Virginia Restaurant at some point in the 1940s or 1950s, after the 1880s structure had already undergone renovations resulting in its appearance in the historic image at left. It was this type of modernization—along with the use of neon signs—that spurred the formation of Colonial Leesburg, Inc., in 1949. (Historic photograph courtesy of the Winslow Williams Photograph Collection [VC 0003], Thomas Balch Library, Leesburg, Virginia.)

Two of the most significant changes that occurred in Leesburg's commercial district in the mid-20th century were the removal of most of the street trees and subsequent narrowing of the sidewalks to accommodate increased automobile traffic and on-street parking. In this view of South King Street, one can clearly see the row of shops punctuated on the north by First National Bank and on the south by the opera house. In fact, this is one of the few view of the opera house in a streetscape context. (Historic photograph courtesy of the Winslow Williams Photograph Collection [VC 0003], Thomas Balch Library, Leesburg, Virginia.)

THE ECONOMIC AND SOCIAL CENTER OF LOUDOUN COUNTY

In this early view of Raflo's, a popular women's clothing store, one can clearly see the design of the storefront prior to its 1930s modernization and eventual removal of the wooden balcony. Though no formal documentation has been found to corroborate it, this structure is likely among the many works (including the Leesburg Inn, on page 28) of the Norris Brothers, a prolific lumber mill on South King Street known for its highly ornamental buildings and interiors (pages 52 and 53). (Historic photograph courtesy of the Winslow Williams Photograph Collection [VC 0003], Thomas Balch Library, Leesburg, Virginia.)

The historic photograph was taken shortly after a fire destroyed the buildings at 23 and 25 South King Street in November 1976. Previously occupied by White's Department Store, by the time of the fire, they housed Nichol's Appliance Center and the Silco Cut Price Store. The new building was constructed in 1977–1978. Though damaged by the fire, the three-story structure at 27 South King Street was restored. (Historic photograph courtesy of the Winslow Williams Photograph Collection [VC 0003], Thomas Balch Library, Leesburg, Virginia.)

THE ECONOMIC AND SOCIAL CENTER OF LOUDOUN COUNTY

By the time this photograph was taken, the two structures at 6–8 Loudoun Street SW, at the far left in the image above, had been altered for use as a commercial building by the removal of the two porches and the consolidation of the two doorways (page 87). In the mid-1980s, the building was removed from Loudoun Street and now sits at 108 Church Street SE. Now renovated, the building at 108 Church Street SE is known as the Tolbert Building. (Historic photograph courtesy of the Town of Leesburg Department of Planning & Zoning.)

Constructed in the 19th century, the board-and-batten-clad frame commercial building on the northwest corner of King and Loudoun Streets was replaced in the 1920s with the current building, reflecting a period of commercial prosperity in the community in the early 20th century. (Historic photograph courtesy of the Town of Leesburg Department of Planning & Zoning)

THE ECONOMIC AND SOCIAL CENTER OF LOUDOUN COUNTY

Now replaced by a mid-20th-century department store that currently houses an antique mall, the Leesburg Opera House was erected in the 1890s. The building featured two commercial storefronts on the ground floor. The opera house was located on the second and third floors, with the entrance through the round-arched doorway to the left of the shops. In the early 20th century, the fire department was in a separate one-story structure behind the opera house. (Historic photograph courtesy of the Winslow Williams Photograph Collection [VC 0003], Thomas Balch Library, Leesburg, Virginia.)

Constructed around 1900, the building at the southeast corner of King and Loudoun Streets has changed little over the past 100 years. The building was added onto an existing mid-19th-century structure facing Loudoun Street and served as a dwelling and the home the Thompson-Plaster X-Ray Company, which occupied the first floor. The main entrance to the business was via Loudoun Street, while the ornamental doorway facing King Street served the residence. By the 1940s, the building housed the local telephone exchange. (Historic photograph courtesy of Historical Postcards, 1900–2008 [VC 0004], Thomas Balch Library, Leesburg, Virginia.)

Thompson-Plaster X Ray Co., King and Loudoun Streets

Although some documentation suggests that this building was constructed in the early 19th century, its cosmetic features and overall appearance date primarily to the 1870s or 1880s, with significant changes to the building's storefronts in the early 20th century. It was likely at that time that the exterior was finished with stucco. Though the historic photograph depicts Breckenridge's Saddle and Collar Shop as well as a Singer sewing machine store, the building housed many different businesses over the years. (Historic photograph courtesy of the Thomas Balch Library Photograph Collection [VC 0001], Thomas Balch Library, Leesburg, Virginia.)

Like many gas stations built in the 1950s, L.S. Hutchinson's new Esso gas station was designed in the Colonial Revival style and complemented the historic character of the community. Although the building has remained much the same over the last 60 years, the surrounding structures have seen many changes. The buildings at 201 South King Street and 1 Royal Street SW, to the right in the image above, have had their mid-to-late-19th-century porches removed. (Historic photograph courtesy of the Winslow Williams Photograph Collection [VC 0003], Thomas Balch Library, Leesburg, Virginia.)

THE ECONOMIC AND SOCIAL CENTER OF LOUDOUN COUNTY

The building at 222 South King Street has changed much over time. Evident to the left in the historic photograph is the brick core of the building, which is the earliest portion of the structure. It was originally built as the Leesburg Electric Light Company's power station in the late 1880s or early 1890s. By 1903, the frame building served as a workshop, most likely for the adjacent Norris Brothers' mill works. By 1930, the structure was converted into the Leesburg Laundry, a dry cleaning business. The front portion of the building was replaced by the current structure in the 1960s. (Historic photograph courtesy of the Winslow Williams Photograph Collection [VC 0003], Thomas Balch Library, Leesburg, Virginia.)

Even as recently as the mid-1940s, nothing but a few small outbuildings occupied the site of the Loudoun County Government Center. The historic dwellings that still face Market Street were the main buildings on this block. In the late 1940s or 1950s, the A&P Food Store and Drug Fair pharmacy was built, with a large paved parking lot covering much of the land. The grocery store existed through the late 20th century, when it was demolished to build the government center. The parking garage now occupies the site of the A&P. (Historic photograph courtesy of the Winslow Williams Photograph Collection [VC 0003], Thomas Balch Library, Leesburg, Virginia.)

THE ECONOMIC AND SOCIAL CENTER OF LOUDOUN COUNTY

Constructed in the early 1800s, the Valley Bank Building was a commercial structure through the early 20th century. In the mid-1900s, it was acquired by Loudoun County for use as additional office space, and it was later renovated in 1987. (Historic photograph courtesy of the Town of Leesburg Department of Planning & Zoning.)

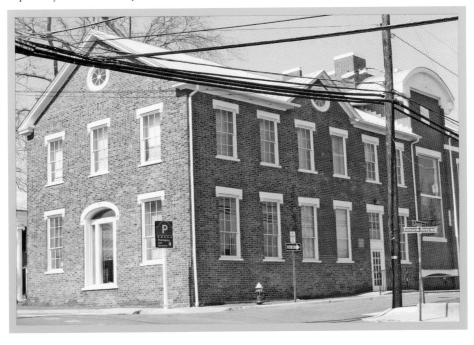

In the 1950s, the iconic structure known as the Mighty Midget Kitchen was installed on a concrete pad to the north of the gas station at Market and Loudoun Streets. Built from an airplane fuselage, the structure was later given a neon sign. The Mighty Midget, as it is popularly known, was removed from this site, restored, and reinstalled at 201 Royal Street SE in the late 20th century (page 66). It now houses the Doner Bistro. (Historic photograph courtesy of the Winslow Williams Photograph Collection [VC 0003], Thomas Balch Library, Leesburg, Virginia.)

THE ECONOMIC AND SOCIAL CENTER OF LOUDOUN COUNTY

# LEESBURG'S MANUFACTURING AND AGRICULTURAL HERITAGE

Very little remains of Leesburg's manufacturing and agricultural buildings, which were once a prominent feature of the historic downtown. Many of the structures have been lost to deterioration and eventual demolition, while others—like this agricultural building—were renovated and reconfigured to create Market Station in the 1980s (page 63). Even through the 1970s, the area around Market Station was underdeveloped and featured unpaved streets and open space. (Historic photograph courtesy of the Thomas Balch Library Photograph Collection [VC 0001], Thomas Balch Library, Leesburg, Virginia.)

This early view of South King Street was taken before 1912 and is one of the only known images of the Norris Brothers Planing Mill, shown to the left and beside the structure that was later the Leesburg Laundry (page 47). The Norris Brothers Planing Mill was responsible for many of the late-19th- and early-20th-century buildings and interior woodwork found throughout Leesburg. Also apparent in the image is the natural location of Town Branch, which may be seen flowing across South King Street and under a bridge between the two structures to the left. (Historic photograph courtesy of the Ethel Littlejohn Adams Photograph Collection [VC 0015], Thomas Balch Library, Leesburg, Virginia.)

The J.T. Hirst Lumber Company buildings were constructed between 1912 and 1930 on the site of the Norris Brothers Planing Mill. The property ceased to be used as a lumber company in the early 1980s. The site has changed significantly in character, particularly due to the demolition of more than half the historic structure for the relocation of Town Branch. In the historic image above, it may be seen to the left of the J.T. Hirst building. The portion of the building to the right in the image was later removed. (Historic photograph courtesy of the Winslow Williams Photograph Collection [VC 0003], Thomas Balch Library, Leesburg, Virginia.)

This passenger station was the second to serve Leesburg, which gained railroad service in 1860. This structure, built in the 1880s or 1890s, existed through the mid-20th century. The relocation of Town Branch, which originally flowed behind the depot and followed a course along South Street, brought the stream closer to the Washington & Old Dominion (W&OD) and over the site of the depot. (Historic photograph courtesy of the Northern Virginia Regional Park Authority, Fairfax Station, Virginia.)

LEESBURG'S MANUFACTURING AND AGRICULTURAL HERITAGE

This freight depot was constructed around 1899, after the first train station burned. Located west of Harrison Street on the site of what is now a row of townhouses, the freight depot was moved to its current site at Market Station in the mid-1980s (page 64). It now houses Fireworks Pizza. (Historic photograph courtesy of the Northern Virginia Regional Park Authority, Fairfax Station, Virginia.)

The Leesburg Lime Kiln Company operated a quarry to the east of the limekilns, remnants of which may still be seen on the W&OD Trail. The quarry was later filled with water as the company moved the quarry to the west of the kilns. In the late 20th century, the quarry was filled, and property became an automobile junkyard. (Historic photograph courtesy of the Northern Virginia Regional Park Authority, Fairfax Station, Virginia.)

Leesburg Lime kilns and Lake.

Between 1936 and 1947, the Leesburg Lime Kiln Company became the Leesburg Lime & Fuel Corporation, which built a large frame complex abutting the kilns. The portion of the structure in the foreground served as shipping, with the taller section housing the elevators. The large concrete structure that still exists today was the crusher. (Historic photograph courtesy of the Northern Virginia Regional Park Authority, Fairfax Station, Virginia.)

This 1980s view facing north along Harrison Street shows the area around Harrison and the W&OD Trail prior to the federally funded redevelopment of this site for the Market Station complex in the mid-1980s. One cannot understate the impact of this project on later development in Leesburg and on the physical landscape of this part of town. (Historic photograph courtesy of the Town of Leesburg Department of Planning & Zoning.)

LEESBURG'S MANUFACTURING AND AGRICULTURAL HERITAGE

Commonly known as the Leesburg stockyards, the Loudoun County Livestock Market was constructed between 1937 and 1946 on the site of one-story agricultural warehouses. The building served as an auction house, and its position near the railroad facilitated the shipping of livestock. The structure burned around 1980. The Morningside assisted living facility was later built on the site. (Historic photograph courtesy of the Northern Virginia Regional Park Authority, Fairfax Station, Virginia.)

Known in the mid-20th century as Buick Street, Harrison Street was the central corridor in Leesburg's agricultural and industrial district. The modest one-story dwelling in the foreground of the historic photograph below was relocated to the northwest corner of Harrison and South Streets at the same time that the Saffer Mill, behind it in the photograph below, was moved to its current site. The dwelling now houses a cigar shop, and the mill has served as the Tuscarora Mill Restaurant since the redevelopment. (Historic photograph courtesy of the Town of Leesburg Department of Planning & Zoning.)

This view of the intersection of South and Church Streets depicts a historic building that was constructed for the J.T. Hirst Lumber Company and later used as a creamery. It was removed after 1975 and replaced with the current office building. (Historic photograph courtesy of the Town of Leesburg Department of Planning & Zoning.)

By October 1985, the warehouse and general store shown in the foreground on the southwest corner of Harrison and South Streets were demolished, making way for the relocation of the Saffer Mill and the dwelling beside it. (Historic photograph courtesy of the Town of Leesburg Department of Planning & Zoning.)

LEESBURG'S MANUFACTURING AND AGRICULTURAL HERITAGE

The only building to be retained in its original position for the Market Station redevelopment, this agricultural implements warehouse was completely renovated in the mid-1980s (page 51). Now anchoring the southwest corner of the development, the building currently houses several businesses. (Historic photograph courtesy of the Thomas Balch Library Photograph Collection [VC 0001], Thomas Balch Library, Leesburg, Virginia.)

In the early 1900s, this was the site of a four-story, 50-foot-tall rolling mill (for which no photograph is known to exist). It was demolished after 1912 and, by 1930, replaced by the Leesburg Grain and Feed Company, pictured below. Although the building was gone by 1975, the grain bins shown in the foreground remained through the 1980s. The bins had a capacity of 4,000 bushels each. (Historic photograph courtesy of the Winslow Williams Photograph Collection [VC 0003], Thomas Balch Library, Leesburg, Virginia.)

Like the Market Station development, the impact of the Loudoun County Government Center on the landscape of downtown Leesburg cannot be overlooked. This five-story office building, constructed in the 1990s, is the largest building in the Old and Historic District and dominates the landscape from every direction. (Historic photograph courtesy of the Town of Leesburg Department of Planning & Zoning.)

The grain and feed warehouse at the corner of Harrison and Royal Streets was significantly renovated in the 1980s for use as a commercial building. The structure is now home to the Mighty Midget Kitchen, which was moved from its former location next to the gas station at Market and Loudoun Streets (page 50). (Historic photograph courtesy of the Town of Leesburg Department of Planning & Zoning.)

The structure in the foreground of this historic photograph served as a feed and hay shop, with a four-car automobile garage attached to the right side of the building. In the background is a blacksmith and woodworking shop that, even in the 1940s, had an earth floor. The structures were removed in the early 2000s for the development of the Leesburg Central project. (Historic photograph courtesy of the Thomas Balch Library Photograph Collection [VC 0001], Thomas Balch Library, Leesburg, Virginia.)

At the north of Leesburg's industrial section was the Leesburg Ice Company. Located near the end of a railroad spur terminating at Loudoun Street, the ice plant was a three-story structure that later became the Frozen Food Locker Company in the 1940s and, by the time this 1975 photograph was taken, the Loudoun Packing Company. Its removal facilitated the development of Market Station. (Historic photograph courtesy of the Town of Leesburg Department of Planning & Zoning.)

CHAPTER

4

# DOMESTIC AND RELIGIOUS BUILDINGS

Leesburg's historic dwellings range in age from the late 1700s through the mid-1950s, with many of the earliest structures serving both commercial and domestic uses. In some cases, the historic dwellings were later altered for use as offices or retail shops, as was the case with the structure in the foreground, which was a house as late as 1946. (Historic photograph courtesy of the Winslow Williams Photograph Collection [VC 0003], Thomas Balch Library, Leesburg, Virginia.)

Leesburg is home to two intersections known as "The Parting of the Ways" (page 77). These images depict the parting on the western end of the historic residential neighborhood. The area where Market Street (left) and Loudoun Street (right) diverge was originally a large field. The property was subdivided in the late 20th century and is now the site of Westgreen, which includes one historic dwelling along West Market Street. (Historic photograph courtesy of Historical Postcards, 1900–2008 [VC 0004], Thomas Balch Library, Leesburg, Virginia.)

Now a busy thoroughfare into downtown Leesburg, West Market Street was, through the mid-1900s, a quiet residential street with little traffic. This photograph was taken on 25 July 1955 on the occasion of an automobile accident at the intersection of West Market and Ayr Streets. (Historic photograph courtesy of the Winslow Williams Photograph Collection [VC 0003], Thomas Balch Library, Leesburg, Virginia.)

One of several companion photographs of the accident shown on the previous page, this image is one of the few historic views of Ayr Street. The building in the foreground was a small, one-story dwelling until it was removed and rebuilt as a two-story structure in 2009. (Historic photograph courtesy of the Winslow Williams Photograph Collection [VC 0003], Thomas Balch Library, Leesburg, Virginia.)

DOMESTIC AND RELIGIOUS BUILDINGS

Like the two preceding images, this photograph depicts the area around West Market and Ayr Streets prior to the development of the Westgreen neighborhood. The dwelling on the southwest corner of Market and Ayr Streets (shown left of center in the photograph below) is another example of the residential in-fill that occurred in downtown Leesburg in the late 20th century. (Historic photograph courtesy of the Winslow Williams Photograph Collection [VC 0003], Thomas Balch Library, Leesburg, Virginia.)

The two attached dwellings at 222 and 224 are among the earliest on West Market Street. The house at 222 West Market Street was constructed around 1850, while 224 West Market Street was built during the first quarter of the 19th century. Both structures were given to the Loudoun Restoration and Preservation Society (now the Loudoun Preservation Society) in the 1970s. Before the organization could renovate the two buildings, 224 West Market (shown at the left) partially collapsed. It was rebuilt over the next two years. (Historic photograph courtesy of the Thomas Balch Library Photograph Collection [VC 0001], Thomas Balch Library, Leesburg, Virginia.)

DOMESTIC AND RELIGIOUS BUILDINGS

Built in the early 1950s, the seven dwellings at Honicon Court are among several developments completed by Claude Honicon in Leesburg in the 1950s. In this March 1954 photograph, the structure at 231 West Market Street was still being completed. Notable in this historic photograph is the absence of tree canopy. Among Honicon's other residential developments are those on Union Street and Edwards Ferry Road. (Historic photograph courtesy of the Winslow Williams Photograph Collection [VC 0003], Thomas Balch Library, Leesburg, Virginia.)

In this earliest known view of East Market Street, directly opposite the Loudoun County Courthouse, are several residential buildings that were demolished in the early 1900s for newer commercial structures, including the post office and the auto showroom depicted on page 34.

The dwelling at right in the photograph below is a rare example of an 18th-century gambrel-roofed building in Leesburg. (Historic photograph courtesy of Historical Postcards, 1900–2008 [VC 0004], Thomas Balch Library, Leesburg, Virginia.)

DOMESTIC AND RELIGIOUS BUILDINGS

Parting of the Ways, East Market and Fayette Streets.    Leesburg, Va.

The parting of East Market and Fayette Streets was historically occupied by a modest two-and-a-half-story dwelling that existed as late as 1947. Built in its place in 1964 was the Barrister Building, an example of mid-20th-century infill office development. (Historic photograph courtesy of Historical Postcards, 1900–2008 [VC 0004], Thomas Balch Library, Leesburg, Virginia.)

This image of 101 North King Street, on the corner of King and Cornwall Streets, shows the building prior to the late-20th-century removal of its porch. Many of Leesburg's late-18th- and early-19th-century buildings were constructed without porches but later had them added as stylistic updates in the late 1800s and early 1900s. The ready availability of lumber and ornamental millwork from the Norris Brothers Planing Mill made such improvements convenient. Many of these porches were removed in the late 1900s. (Historic photograph courtesy of the Winslow Williams Photograph Collection [VC 0003], Thomas Balch Library, Leesburg, Virginia.)

DOMESTIC AND RELIGIOUS BUILDINGS

With additions constructed around 1816, 1896, and 1932, the brick section of this dwelling is the oldest and dates to the 1760s. In the early 1800s, it served as a parsonage for the adjacent Methodist meetinghouse (page 80), and it housed a community library in the early 1900s. Today, the house is the rectory for St. James Episcopal Church. (Historic photograph courtesy of the Thomas Balch Library Research Visual Collection [VC 0002], Thomas Balch Library, Leesburg, Virginia.)

The property on the northeast corner of Cornwall and Liberty Streets is significant in many ways. Purchased by the Methodist Church in 1766, it is the earliest Methodist-owned property in the United States. The stone meetinghouse was constructed around 1790 as the first Methodist church in Virginia. The structure fell into disrepair and was demolished in the early 20th century. (Historic photograph courtesy of Historical Postcards, 1900–2008 [VC 0004], Thomas Balch Library, Leesburg, Virginia.)

DOMESTIC AND RELIGIOUS BUILDINGS

SE IN WHICH WM WIRT ONCE LIVED
VIRT ST., LEESBURG, VA.

This view of the house at 12 Wirt Street NW was taken before 1907. When first built, the structure was a one-and-a-half-story stone dwelling with dormer windows facing Wirt Street. At some point between 1907 and 1912, the structure was increased in height to two stories, which was not uncommon for small masonry buildings in Leesburg. Another such example exists at 112 Edwards Ferry Road. (Historic photograph courtesy of Historical Postcards, 1900–2008 [VC 0004], Thomas Balch Library, Leesburg, Virginia.)

DOMESTIC AND RELIGIOUS BUILDINGS

As illustrated by this mid-20th-century photograph, the block of Wirt Street between Market and Loudoun Streets has changed little over the past 150 years. Though most of the buildings have been renovated or restored, the historic character embodied by this streetscape remains intact. (Historic photograph courtesy of the Winslow Williams Photograph Collection [VC 0003], Thomas Balch Library, Leesburg, Virginia.)

DOMESTIC AND RELIGIOUS BUILDINGS

Small vernacular dwellings, particularly those dating to the 19th and early 20th centuries, have not fared as well as many of the larger houses in town. The small house at 203 Liberty Street SW, pictured below in 1975, was one of two that were demolished in the 1980s for construction of this two-and-a-half-story commercial building. It was at roughly this time that the large multiunit residential development at Chesterfield Place, which forms the backdrop for the new structure, was also built. (Historic photograph courtesy of the Town of Leesburg Department of Planning & Zoning.)

The stone dwelling at 106 Loudoun Street SW was constructed in the 1760s and was not, contrary to local legend, a temporary headquarters of George Washington during the Seven Years' War. Historically, there were two small frame dwellings between this house and the structure on the corner of Loudoun and Wirt Streets. A portion of one may be seen at the right in the photograph below. Both buildings were demolished in the mid-1900s, and the stone building was renovated in the 1960s. It was likely around this time that the late-1800s porch was also removed. (Historic photograph courtesy of Historical Postcards, 1900–2008 [VC 0004], Thomas Balch Library, Leesburg, Virginia.)

Washington's Headquarters, Loudoun Street
Leesburg, Va.

DOMESTIC AND RELIGIOUS BUILDINGS

Built between 1912 and 1930 and pictured above in 1975, the house at 105 Loudoun Street SW was demolished in the 1970s for construction of a companion commercial building to the stone structure at 103 Loudoun Street (page 69). In the early 1900s, the historic dwelling featured a full-width one-story porch facing Loudoun Street. (Historic photograph courtesy of the Town of Leesburg Department of Planning & Zoning.)

Of particular note in Leesburg's downtown residential neighborhood is this recently identified photograph of the house that stood at the intersection of Loudoun and Wirt Streets. Constructed between 1894 and 1899, this Queen Anne–style house was probably the work of Norris Brothers (page 52). If so, it rivals all of their other buildings from the late 19th century in Leesburg. Anecdotal accounts suggest that the tower was struck by lightning in the 1930s and subsequently demolished. The remainder of the house was torn down in the mid-20th century. The current building dates to the late 1900s. (Historic photograph courtesy of the Thomas Balch Library Photograph Collection [VC 0001], Thomas Balch Library, Leesburg, Virginia.)

DOMESTIC AND RELIGIOUS BUILDINGS

This view of Loudoun Street SE was taken around 1950, at the time that Colonial Leesburg, Inc., sponsored the installation of the brick sidewalks downtown. The 18th- and 19th-century structures along Loudoun Street were demolished in the 1950s and early 1960s. Almost all of these buildings were residential at the time of this photograph, reinforcing the fact that Leesburg had a thriving residential neighborhood at the heart of downtown well into the 20th century. (Historic photograph courtesy of the Winslow Williams Photograph Collection [VC 0003], Thomas Balch Library, Leesburg, Virginia.)

This turn-of-the-20th-century dwelling was one of two vacant buildings that were removed in the 1970s and replaced by the multiunit Colonial Square office development. The other dwelling was also frame and closely resembled the existing building at 106 Edwards Ferry Road. (Historic photograph courtesy of the Town of Leesburg Department of Planning & Zoning.)

DOMESTIC AND RELIGIOUS BUILDINGS

Similar to the fate of the house on page 83, this dwelling near the intersection of Church and North Streets was built in the early 1900s and demolished around 1980. It was replaced by the two attached townhouses shown below. (Historic photograph courtesy of the Town of Leesburg Department of Planning & Zoning.)

Like the impact of the Market Station development in the 1980s and the Loudoun County Government Center in the 1990s, the changes resulting from the Loudoun County Courts expansion have been significant. The three early-20th-century dwellings at the intersection of Church and Cornwall Streets were used as county offices until being demolished in the late 1990s for the construction of the new courts complex. (Historic photograph courtesy of the Town of Leesburg Department of Planning & Zoning.)

DOMESTIC AND RELIGIOUS BUILDINGS

Lending its name to Church Street, St. James Episcopal Church was first built in 1812 and then replaced by a new structure in the 1830s. Pictured here is the second building, which was designed in a transitional Gothic Revival/Italianate style. The congregation moved to its current Romanesque Revival–style building at the intersection of Cornwall and Wirt Streets in 1895. (Historic photograph courtesy of the Winslow Williams Photograph Collection [VC 0003], Thomas Balch Library, Leesburg, Virginia.)

This view southwest of South King Street clearly shows the almost rural nature of the southern end of the town in the early 20th century. At the time this photograph was taken, this area was the edge of town and nearly the end of the residential development before entering Loudoun County. (Historic photograph courtesy of Historical Postcards, 1900–2008 [VC 0004], Thomas Balch Library, Leesburg, Virginia.)

South King Street. Leesburg, Va

DOMESTIC AND RELIGIOUS BUILDINGS

Looking North on South King Street.    Leesburg, Va.

Most of the houses on South King Street date to the late 1800s and early 1900s and represent a later phase of residential development in Leesburg. Interestingly, the east and west sides of South King Street follow very different development patterns. Those on the west side are larger estates, while those on the east side of the street are smaller and closer together. (Historic photograph courtesy of Historical Postcards, 1900–2008 [VC 0004], Thomas Balch Library, Leesburg, Virginia.)

DOMESTIC AND RELIGIOUS BUILDINGS

"Carlheim", Residence of Mrs. R. A. Paxton, Leesburg, Va.

Carlheim, located to the northeast of Leesburg's downtown core, was one of the largest estates in the area at the time it was built in the 1870s. The property included nearly all of what is now the Exeter neighborhood and featured, in addition to this Second Empire–style house, a stone smokehouse, peacock house, and several barns. The Exeter neighborhood's community center on Fieldstone Drive and the outbuildings at Red Rock Wilderness Park on Edwards Ferry Road were once part of the estate. Now held by trustees, the property is home to the Arc of Loudoun. (Historic photograph courtesy of Historical Postcards, 1900–2008 [VC 0004], Thomas Balch Library, Leesburg, Virginia.)

Domestic and Religious Buildings

The property for which the Exeter neighborhood was named faced a different fate from Carlheim (page 94). Built in the mid-1700s, Exeter was one of the earliest and grandest buildings in the area around Leesburg. It was a place of social prominence through the late 19th century. By the time the house burned in the 1980s, the property had been part of a large annexation into the town. The ruins were later demolished to facilitate commercial development along Edwards Ferry Road. (Historic photograph courtesy of the Loudoun Museum, Leesburg, Virginia.)

# www.arcadiapublishing.com

MAP SEARCH

Discover books about the town where you grew up, the cities where your friends and families live, the town where your parents met, or even that retirement spot you've been dreaming about. Our Web site provides history lovers with exclusive deals, advanced notification about new titles, e-mail alerts of author events, and much more.

Find Your Place in History.